DONALD TRUMP'S
COMEBACK GIG

by

Acknowledgements

I would like to thank my wife and our two girls who always proved to be a great source of encouragement when I was authoring this book. Had it not been for their support, we would not be where we are today. It with humility of heart that I thank them for continuously being there when their support was needed.

I dedicate this book to all my friends and family. And to those who enjoy reading about world politics, with the American scene in particular. It is my hope that you will find this book to be of interest.

Thank you.

Preface

Following the results of the 2020 election, a lot has been

said about what the future holds for former President Donald Trump. While refusing to accept the legitimacy of the results of the 2020 election, Trump's future has been shrouded in mystery. His political opponents still fear him, and there has been a reluctance from mainstream Republicans when it comes to condemning certain actions of his that are known to be just plain wrong. This reluctance shows how much of an effect Donald Trump still has on the Republican base.

This book will analyze how we ended up in this scenario. We will be examining how Trump came to be elected as President and what tactics he employed in order to reach the Whitehouse. Moreover, the following questions will also be examined:

1. Why was Trump appealing for traditional Republican voters?

2. Was the Trump presidency a successful presidency?

3. And most importantly, will Trump aim to run for President again in 2024?

The first question will be answered in Chapter 1 and 2. The third question on the other hand will be analyzed deeply in Chapter 2, while Chapter 3 and 4 will focus on what a potential 2024 run for Trump would look like, if it takes place at all.

While acknowledging that it's been exciting writing this book, I also encourage you to stay up to date with the latest news and to delve into the matter as much as possible. You are encouraged to continue researching and reading about these subject and similar ones. And you are also encouraged to analyze past events and look out for future trends. For at the end of the day it is only by doing the latter that we can find the answers of the future.

Chapter 1. The run up to 2016

When announcing his run for President in 2015, few were the commentators who took Donald Trump seriously. John Oliver, the liberal host of HBO's Last Week Tonight had said he'd pay Trump to run. Then President Barack Obama had humiliated Trump in 2011 at the Whitehouse Correspondents' Dinner, going so far as to joke that Trump would turn the Whitehouse into a hotel with its own casino and golf course. According to Trump's former associate Omarosa Manigault Newman it was this latter event, that made the Donald's mind up about running for President.

Trump sees himself as a strong man. And he wanted to manifest his strength to the world. The 2016 election is insightful in as much as it shows how a man's perseverance and determination can defy all the odds and propel him to becoming President of the United States. This is especially true, since Trump himself ran against a dynasty – a political machine which had been sustaining itself for decades. This did not stop him however, from employing tactics which shifted the battlefield to his favour.

In fact Trump's strength and appeal came from the fact that he is considered to be a disruptor. Everyone recognizes his disruptive capabilities, and everyone knew that Trump had been mulling a run. Yet no one prepared for what was to come. No one prepared for Trump's eventual rise. This was more than seen when Trump schooled Senator Lindsey Graham by giving away his phone number at a rally after Sen. Graham called him a "jackass". Or when he humiliated Jeb Bush during a Republican Presidential debate by shushing the former   Governor.

Not to mention the fact that Trump is virtually the only

Presidential contender who was ever capable of winning a debate, even when the staunchly mainstream Republican audience booed him over and over. And how did he do this? By constantly countering. When the audience booed him, he countered "That's all of his [Jeb Bush's] donors and special interests out there." Now I myself was watching this debate at this very moment and I remember thinking to myself: "damn, this is something that only happens once in a lifetime." This moment would stay in my mind. And it would stay in my mind even more so because this same tactic of constant countering would be employed by Trump throughout the 2016 campaign.

When Secretary Clinton, the 2016 Democratic nominee, stated in the second Presidential debate that it was awfully good that someone like Donald Trump is not President, Trump countered by saying "Yeah, because you'd be in jail", to the audience's laughter. Trump went into that debate as the underdog. It's unclear how he went out of it however. What we know for certain is that he won the 2016 election, albeit by losing the popular vote. However, rules are rules. And the American constitution is clear in stating that he or she who get the most electoral votes become the President of the United States. At the end of the day, that is what happened on the 20th of January of 2017 when Donald J. Trump was inaugurated as the 45th President of the United States.

Chapter 2. Trump's Presidency 2017-2021

Winning the Presidential election by consolidating his support in swing states, most notably the three mid-Western states of Wisconsin, Michigan and Pennsylvania (which had not went for a Republican since 1988), Trump became President on the 20th of January 2017. His message as regards to the economy and trade are what many analysts believe lead to his victory in these states, with traditionally Democrat blue-collar workers voting for Trump as they perceived him to be anti-globalization. And when their jobs were being shipped to Mexico or China, a globalist candidate would be the last person that these Mid-Western folks would vote for.

In analysing Trump's performance as President, we shall be looking at his policies on a sector by sector basis. Starting with the economic and healthcare sectors is only fair, since these are the two sectors which have been tremendously affected by the pandemic. Then we'll be moving towards trade, migration, and race which were all hot potatoes during Trump's term in office. Finally, we will be finishing up with foreign policy.

2.1 The Economy

In Trump's first three years, America saw unprecedented economic growth. Unemployment was at an all-time low, the stock market at an all-time high, and business was booming. Yet in the beginning of 2020, the coronavirus pandemic struck, and what had been a prosperous time turned into a complete nightmare. As lockdowns were implemented in various states, people started losing their jobs. And while those working in certain economic niches such as the digitalized economy gained plentifully in 2020, the same cannot be said for the vast majority of Americans who were working in traditional economic sectors.

Going by the Keynesian mantra, Trump and the Republican congress sent cheques to every American family in order to cushion the pandemic's economic impact. There is no doubt that such a measure was well warranted – economically speaking, direct money in people's hands is more effective than tax breaks. Therefore, this policy was a good policy.

Yet were the amounts that were sent enough? The answer to this question of course is no. That being said, it would be unfair to put this blame solely on Trump, as it is more likely that the Republican congress pulled the break on larger cheques being sent out. Traditionally, Republicans are more predisposed towards tax-breaks when dealing with economic crises, while Democrats are more predisposed towards more public spending programmes. And the fact that Trump is not, so to speak, a *"traditional Republican"* makes it more likely than not that he recognized the need for more aid. In fact, Trump had said so in public on multiple occasions, including in December 2020, that he wanted to send $2000 stimulus cheques to every home.

2.2 Healthcare

The American healthcare system needs no introduction. Contrary to other industrialized nations in the world,

America's system is a privatized one. It differs greatly to the United Kingdom's healthcare system – the National Health Service or the NHS, which guarantees healthcare as a right for all Brits. In fact, if you're an American without healthcare insurance, you'll have two options if you get sick: either stay sick or rake up thousands of dollars of medical debt.

Trump's attempts at reforming America's healthcare were quite disappointing. He tried multiple times to repeal Obamacare in order to replace it with a plan of his own. And he failed each and every time. Meanwhile, virtually nothing was done which guarantees healthcare for the uninsured 30 million American citizens, most of which are poor and working-class folks who cannot afford insurance.

The latter fact came to bite the U.S. in the back when the coronavirus hit American shores. While the whole world struggled with covid19, America's pandemic management was a gross failure. As of this moment, the United States is fast approaching 30 million covid19 cases with over half a million deaths – ranking first globally in both deaths and covid19 cases. Surely, that is a statistic that no American can ever be proud of, especially if they were the sitting President of the United States when the pandemic was raging.

2.3 Trade

During the Presidential campaign, Trump had said over and over again that China was killing America when it comes to trade. Trump's Whitehouse kept this in mind when dealing with China so much so that a so called "trade-war" started in 2018 with the Trump administration imposing tariffs on Chinese products and setting up various trade barriers. In this regard, Trump was seen as wielding protectionist principles in order to protect American trade.

Moreover, Trump also employed Professor Peter

Navarro as Director of the Office of Trade and Manufacturing Policy within the Whitehouse. Those who have followed Peter Navarro's writings and career, know that he's quite bullish on China. He never misses an opportunity to attack the flooding of Chinese goods in America, which he argues, hurt American businesses. And Navarro's appointment was very reflective in the way the Trump administration acted on China.

Another reason for Trump's bullish stance on China was his blue-collar support in the Mid-West. Trump needed Wisconsin, Michigan, and Pennsylvania to get re-elected and he knew that the trade message would resonate in these states. Unfortunately for Trump however, this message did not resonate enough, and in 2020 he ran against Joe Biden (who was born in Scranton, Pennsylvania), and not Hillary Clinton, who was very much seen as being part of the north east's liberal elite.

2.4 Race

Trump's four years as President will be remembered as some of the worse years for African Americans. As can be attested from the what happened to George Floyd and the aftermath of his killing, inequality, racism, and police brutality are still very much present in American society. And these concepts are not just present, they disproportionately affect African Americans in their daily lives. It does not take a genius to recognize that Trump has failed when it comes to race.

That being said, data has shown that Trump does well with a relevant segment of Latino voters (especially Florida Latino voters – the bulk of which are descendants of Cuban exiles).

2.5 Migration

It can be considered ironic that Trump would do well with Florida Latinos when his anti-migration rhetoric is disproportionately focused on Latinos trying to enter the U.S. from its southern border. Ironic as it may seem, it is very much what has happened. During his time in office, Trump continued to be tough on migration. However, his electoral pledge of building a border wall did not happen – and neither did Mexico want to pay for it. Instead former Trump associates such as Steve Bannon launched crowdfunding campaigns in order to be able to finance the building of a border wall. Later on, Bannon would be investigated for alleged money laundering and wire fraud in relation to this crowdfunding campaign – only to be pardoned by Trump before the latter left office.

Of particular interest is also Trump's Executive Order 13780. It must be remembered that during the 2016 campaign Trump had said that he wanted to ban Muslims from entering the United States. And this Executive Order, although not specifically targeting Muslims, was seen by Trump's base as Trump keeping a promise that he had made. Travelling restrictions were at some points during Trump's Presidency in place on the following list of countries:

- Iran;
- Libya;
- Somalia;
- Sudan;
- Syria;
- Yemen;
- Chad;
- North Korea;
- Venezuela;
- Eritrea;
- Kyrgyzstan;
- Myanmar;
- Nigeria; and
- Tanzania.

As can be noted when viewing these countries, a considerable number of them are Muslim-majority countries. And hence it is obvious why Trump's base was content with this Executive Order.

2.6 Foreign Policy

Trump's foreign policy between 2017 and 2021 is testament to the fact that Presidents are very limited when it comes to changing the country's foreign policy. Other players such as the State Department and the Department of Defence play perhaps a more important and pertinent role than the President, who is unable to micro-manage day to day affairs.

This was very much seen with Trump's relations with various "strong-men" such as Russia's Putin, Turkey's Erdogan and Brazil's Bolsonaro. While with the latter two Trump had room for manoeuvre, the same cannot be said as regards Russia. And although the relationship between Trump and Putin arguably was a comfortable and friendly one, it cannot be stated that this also applied to the general American-Russian relationship between the two nations.

On a multilateral level, Trump was a no-show. In fact, Trump took America out of the Paris Agreement, turning his back on climate change – an issue that can only be tackled by global collaboration. He also harshly criticized the World Health Organization multiple times during the coronavirus pandemic. His foreign policy can therefore be characterized as falling within the scope of "radical unilateralism".

This does not mean however, that he did not have his fair share of success. In fact, his ability to pivot 360 degrees from attacking North Korea's Kim Jong-un on twitter, to meeting up with him in North Korea in the span of months is testament to Trump's flexibility. Unfortunately, a deal when it comes to North Korean non-proliferation could not be reached. But everyone agrees that arguably more progress had been made than at any time in the past as regards North Korea.

Chapter 3. A Potential Run in 2024

In this Chapter and Chapter 4, we'll be discussing a potential run by Trump in 2024. Yet this possibility would not have been there, had Trump been convicted after the U.S. Senate after being impeached by the House of Representatives. The Democratic House impeached Trump twice – in 2019 after Trump allegedly tried to force Ukraine President Volodymyr Zelensky to investigate Joe Biden's family dealings in Ukraine, and in 2021, after Trump's supporters invaded Capitol Hill while congress was verifying the 2020 presidential election results. He was acquitted by the Senate in both cases. Had he been convicted (which is always a highly unlikely scenario, given the votes needed for a conviction), Trump could have been barred from running for public office again.

Therefore it goes without saying that the lack of conviction means that Trump is able to run again in 2024. In February of 2021, he even teased a 2024 run when speaking at the Conservative Political Action Conference (CPAC). That being said, there are various issues which must be addressed in order to be able to clear the way for a potential run.

First things first, following the Capitol hill riots, Trump was permanently banned from Twitter. And Twitter was very valuable for Donald Trump – more than it is to other politicians. Twitter was weaponized by Trump and most probably had it not been for his Twitter account, he would not have been elected as President. And therefore, if Trump is to run again, he needs to replace his *"Twitter effect"* with something else. Perhaps this could be another platform. Perhaps it could be another social medium. Yet as of this moment, no one knows what the future holds in this regard.

Secondly, Trump's refusal to acknowledge the results of the 2020 election does not sit well with ordinary and independent American voters. His supporter's Capitol Hill riots sting deeply especially in relation to his "law and order" message. And therefore, it is hard to imagine American independents supporting him again, as they did in droves in 2016. Yet, Trump does have a loyal base, and in the next Chapter we shall be examining where this loyal base can go in 2024.

Thirdly, there are multiple elephants in the room. And these elephants in the room are the investigations currently haunting Trump's personal affairs. His business dealings, his tax returns, and even his conduct in office are all under the microscope of state and federal investigators. And if charges are to be brought against him and his associates, it is more likely than not that his future ambitions will be thwarted. Perhaps this was one of the reasons why Trump was allegedly considering pardoning himself and three of his children (Donald Jr., Ivanka and Eric Trump) before leaving office. This however, he did not do. And therefore, there is no question in stating that he, his children and his associates can be prosecuted both at a federal and at a state level if evidence of wrongdoing is found.

Chapter 4. Hypothetical scenarios

Trump is still relatively popular among his conservative base. The 2021 CPAC straw poll results show Trump leading the Republican field when it comes to a potential 2024 run. While Trump placed first with 55%, Florida Governor Ron De Santis came in second with 21%. 4% on the other hand said that they would vote for South Dakota Governor Kristi Noem.

The CPAC straw poll therefore places Ron De Santis as the only credible challenger vis-à-vis Trump. Yet would De Santis risk running against Trump? That is a question that cannot be answered at this moment in time. And neither can other questions be answered. Questions which include what Trump loyalist Senator Josh Hawley will do with his political future – will he opt to run? And what about former Presidential contender Senator Ted Cruz? It is no secret that the latter has Presidential ambitions.

We would do well however, to keep in mind that the

Republican dynamic is not the only dynamic that will shape the 2024 election. In fact, one still has to see whether Joe Biden will opt to run for a second term. Speculations have long been in circulation that Vice President Kamala Harris will take up the reigns in 2024, with Biden opting for retirement. That being said, if Biden doesn't run for a second term, the Democrats might very well end up with a dividing primary election.

Popular progressive firebrand Congresswoman Alexandria Ocasio Cortez will turn 35 in 2024, thereby making her eligible to run for President in the 2024 election. She'd provide a formidable challenge to any potential Presidential candidate, including to Vice President Kamala Harris. So would current Transportation Secretary and former Presidential Candidate Pete Buttigieg, who is very much seen as a rising star in Democratic ranks.

Therefore, while the door has been closing on Trump ever since he lost the 2020 election, one must admit that the 2024 door has not closed once and for all for his ambitions. In fact, the door is still slightly open, giving Trump enough room to manoeuvre a potential third run. How that will turn out, remains to be seen – but it is certainly **a possibility**.

Chapter 5. All is well that ends well

There are various reasons which might influence Trump to run in 2024. According to former Whitehouse Communications Director Anthony Scaramucci, a potential third run could enable Trump to milk more money from his loyal supporter base, even if his campaigns doesn't last till the end of the primary season. Moreover, a potential run could also signal a show of force to sceptical Republicans – in case the latter try to turn their backs on him and his family.

Punishment would then await those who put Trump under the bus. It is no secret that rumours are already circling about the Trump clan planning to primary Republican legislators who do not support their beloved former President. It's relatively too early to tell whether these threats will be effective.

One thing is for certain however – and that is that for now at least, the Republican Party has become Donald Trump's Party. And if this is to change, then very radical reforms have to take place in the next 4 years.

Various issues come into play in this regard. But instead of examining an endless list of potential issues, perhaps it is better to wait out the storm for a year or two in order to have a better shot at making the correct predictions for 2024. At the end of the day, all is well that ends well, and whatever decision Trump takes going forward, it will undoubtedly be the decision which is in his and his family's **best interest**.

Made in the USA
Las Vegas, NV
06 March 2021

18993397R20015